Plant
Life

ROOTS
AND
SHOOTS

Judith Heneghan and Diego Moscato

WAYLAND

First published in Great Britain in 2015 by Wayland

Copyright © Wayland, 2015

Editor: Nicola Edwards
Designer Anthony Hannant, Little Red Ant

ISBN: 978 0 7502 8767 8
Library eBook ISBN: 978 0 7502 8768 5
Dewey number: 571.8'62-dc23

10 9 8 7 6 5 4 3 2 1

Wayland, an imprint of
Hachette Children's Group
Part of Hodder and Stoughton
Carmelite House
50 Victoria Embankment
London EC4Y 0DZ

An Hachette UK Company
www.hachette.co.uk
www.hachettechildrens.co.uk

Printed and bound in China

MIX
Paper from
responsible sources
FSC® C104740
FSC
www.fsc.org

Contents

All around the world, plants grow in amazing variety. Roots seek out water and anchor the plant. Shoots support the leaves. Read on to discover the extraordinary ways in which roots and shoots spread out to find what each plant needs.

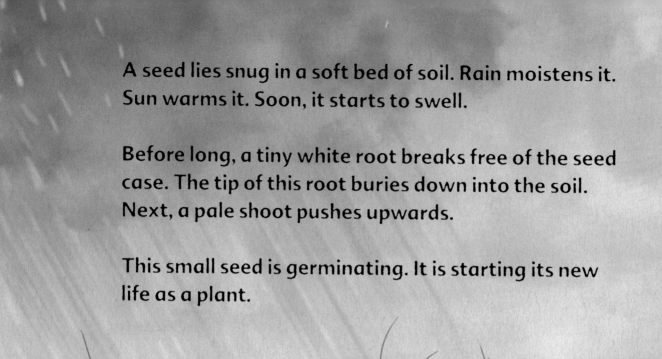

A seed lies snug in a soft bed of soil. Rain moistens it. Sun warms it. Soon, it starts to swell.

Before long, a tiny white root breaks free of the seed case. The tip of this root buries down into the soil. Next, a pale shoot pushes upwards.

This small seed is germinating. It is starting its new life as a plant.

A seed needs warmth and moisture to germinate. It also needs oxygen from the air. So if the soil is too wet or too dry or too cold, the seed cannot grow.

The seeds of this Scots Pine tree lie in frozen ground. They wait for spring, when the sun warms the earth and the snow melts into water.

Under the ground, the new root grows tiny hairs, called rootlets. These rootlets absorb water and nutrients from the soil.

Above the ground, the shoot grows its first green leaves. The seed has become a seedling.

Some seeds wait for up to thirty years for the rain they need to germinate and grow.

Death Valley in California is one of the driest places on Earth. Yet every few years, enough rain falls to soften the tough coats of desert seeds. When this happens, the landscape bursts into life.

Plants like these Mexican gold poppies must germinate, send out roots and shoots, flower and produce new seeds in a few short weeks.

Four months after germinating, this sunflower plant has grown two metres tall. Its shoot is now a sturdy stem that supports the leaves and flowers. The stem helps the leaves and flowers reach the light.

Its root has spread out into web of fine roots. It anchors the plant in the ground.

The leaves and flowers need water. So the stem's other job is to bring water up from the roots. This water travels along narrow tubes inside the stem. Without this water, the leaves would wilt and the plant would quickly die.

A bindweed shoot grows quickly. It is too spindly to support its leaves on its own. So it winds itself around a different plant. Now it can raise its leaves up to the light.

This wild cucumber plant is growing in a wood. It sends out thin shoots called tendrils that wave through the air. When a tendril touches another plant it holds on tight and twists into a coil. This pulls the rest of the plant along behind it.

When lots of plants grow close together, leaves struggle in the shade. The shoots that grow tallest or fastest give their leaves the best chance of reaching the sunlight.

13

A blackberry bramble grows dense and tangled along the edge of a wood. Its thrusting shoots can grow up to ten centimetres each day.

Its stems have sharp prickles that point backwards, like hooks. These hooks help the plant scramble over anything that gets in its way.

When a bramble shoot comes into contact with the ground it sprouts new rootlets that take hold in the soil. In this way, a single bramble can quickly dominate a patch of land.

Roots as well as shoots have adapted to survive in different conditions.

Rainfall is scarce in the dry deserts of Namibia.
So the camel thorn tree grows a long root called a tap root that pushes down through the earth.
In this way it finds water stored deep underground.

Camel thorn tap roots can burrow
downwards for up to sixty metres.

The baobab tree has also adapted to survive in dry conditions. It stores water in its thick, wide trunk.

17

There's no lack of water in the forests of Costa Rica. Here it rains every day. So tree roots spread out just beneath the surface where the soil is rich with nutrients.

But trees with shallow roots are in danger of toppling over. So they also grow surface roots called buttress roots. These tall buttress roots curve out from the trunk. They keep the tree propped up.

The winding shapes of buttress roots also trap leaves and animal droppings. These help enrich the soil.

This orchid grows high in a tree branch in Hawaii. It doesn't need to anchor itself to the ground. Instead its pale roots cling to the tree trunk. These roots absorb moisture from the damp, mist-filled air.

Orchids grow on host trees. They use the host tree's extra height to help their leaves reach the light.

20

The strangler fig also germinates in the branches of trees. Its leaves grow up to the light, while its roots grow down to the ground. These roots wrap themselves around the trunk of the host tree and may even kill it.

22

This Indian Banyan tree is a type of fig. Its roots hang down like long rope, or hair.

23

Most roots grow downwards. Yet some roots grow upwards!

The black mangrove grows in sea-salty swamps. Its roots lie underwater. So the roots sprout rootlets that poke out of the mud. These rootlets take in air through tiny holes.

Oxygen from the air helps roots absorb water and grow. The roots of most plants find the oxygen they need in tiny spaces in the soil. But waterlogged soil contains no air.

24

25

Some plants seem to die back in the cold winter months, but really they are saving their energy. Tulips and daffodils store food in an underground bulb. The bulb sends up new shoots in the spring.

The carrots we eat are really extra wide tap roots.

A potato is an underground storage shoot called a tuber.

This giant redwood tree reaches up into the sky. Its trunk is protected by thick, spongy bark. Its roots spread wide, tangling together beneath the soil with the roots of other trees.

Redwoods can live to be two thousand years old. They are some of the tallest plants in the world. Yet each tree begins as a single root and a shoot.

Plants need roots and shoots to support their leaves, flowers and new seeds.

Things to do

Grow your own seedlings! Cress is quick to germinate and good to eat. First, sprinkle a thin layer of soil on a plate. Then moisten the soil with some water. Next, sprinkle some cress seeds lightly and evenly over the damp soil. Place the plate on a windowsill where there is plenty of sunlight, and in a couple of days the seeds will start to germinate. Remember to keep the soil moist.

In ten days you will have some cress seedlings ready to cut and wash and eat. They are delicious sprinkled across a slice of fresh pizza!

Germination laboratory

One way to observe the growth of both roots and shoots is to make a germination laboratory. All you need is a bean, a clear glass jar and some paper towels.

- Line the inside of the jar with several paper towels.
- Add two to three centimetres of water. The towels will soak up the water.
- Take the bean and tuck it between the paper and the glass, about half way down the jar.
- Place it on a warm windowsill.
- Watch the root grow down while the shoot grows up towards the light.

After two weeks, you should see the first leaves appear. Now you can take it out of the jar and plant it in a pot of soil.

Glossary

bark — outside layer of tree trunk; protects trunk from fire and disease

bulb — an underground storage stem that helps some plants survive the winter

buttress roots — tree roots that grow on the surface to prop up the tree

germination — when a seed starts to grow a root and a shoot

host tree — a tree that is used by another plant

nutrients — substances in the soil that a plant needs for healthy growth

rootlets — hairs or small roots that sprout from the main roots

seedling — a young plant with a root and its first pair of leaves

stem — a shoot that supports leaves and flowers

tap root — a long deep root

tendrils — thin shoots that coil around other plants

tubers — bulging underground roots for storing energy

Further information

The tallest tree in the world is a coast redwood tree, nicknamed Hyperion. It grows in California and measures 115.72 metres tall.

One of the oldest seeds to germinate is a date palm seed found during excavations at Masada in Israel. The seed had been buried amongst the rocks for 2000 years. Scientists planted the seed and, eight weeks later, it sprouted a root and a shoot.

The fastest growing shoot comes from a type of bamboo that can grow up to 90 centimetres in a single day. That's just under one millimetre every 90 seconds!

See what else you can discover about these amazing plants.

Index